Bells
of
Speech

Bells
of
Speech

Nazand Begikhani

Here from Elsewhere

AB

First published in 2006 by Ambit Books,
17 Priory Gardens, London N6 5QY, UK
Publisher: Martin Bax
© 2006 by Nazand Begikhani
Cover image © 2006 by Vanessa Jackson
The moral rights of the author and artist are asserted in
accordance with the Copyright, Designs and Patent Act, 1988

All rights reserved. No part of this publication may be reproduced,
stored in a retrieval system, or transmitted, in any form or by any means,
electronic, mechanical, photocopying, recording or otherwise without the prior
permission in writing of the publisher.

ISBN 0-900055-11-1
ISBN 978-0-900055-11-9

Designed by John Morgan studio
Cover image by Vanessa Jackson
Printed in Great Britain by The Lavenham Press
Distributed by Central Books
The publisher acknowledges the financial assistance of Arts Council England

For my mother Rehan, my sister Awaz and my son Nawzad

Acknowledgements

Acknowledgements are due to the editors of the following magazines and anthologies where these poems first appeared: *Mother Tongue: Modern Poetry in Translation, Salzburg Poetry Review, Poetry Review, Passerelles (in French), Exiled Writers' Ink, Ambit, Crossing the Border, The Silver Throat of the Moon, Modern Kurdish Poetry: An Anthology and Introduction* and *The Fleeing Garden*.

Most of these poems were written in English. Some of them have been translated from Kurdish by the author. Kemal Mirawdali and Stephen Watts translated 'A Song for my People', published in the anthology of *Modern Kurdish Poetry* and Choman Hardi translated 'Question', which appeared in the first issue of *Exiled Writers' Ink*.

I owe special thanks to the following people: Richard McKane, my first English reader and mentor. Jennifer Langer for the creation of the *Exiled Writers' Ink* space. Moniza Alvi whose valuable comments and discussion have been priceless. Jeni Williams for her sincere remarks. Finally, many thanks to my family, Nawzad and John, for support, time and space.

Introduction

Time flows or runs through Nazand Begikhani's poems: the stream of her childhood becomes the mighty river Tigris then she finds herself washed up in exile on the Atlantic ocean, or by the banks of the Loire.

But she is not prepared to just float with the current of the times or tradition. In her poems she fights with the Anfal, the genocidal campaign carried out against Kurdish civilians at the end of the 80s; she fights against honour killings and she fights for the perception of the Kurds in the West. These are painful poems: but pain expressed, of women, of the Kurdish peoples, above all needs to be witnessed by poets and their readers: the politicians of all hues, western and eastern, have let down the Kurds, the armies opposed by the guerrilla movements have neither achieved unity. It is to the exiled Kurdish poets Sherko Bekas, Nazand Begikhani and the younger poet Choman Hardi that we must turn for the true voices (and now in English) of the Kurds, almost to their moral philosophy in a world that is without it, in the same way as one day Osip Mandelstam's work will outlive Stalin. The dictator who oppressed the Kurds in recent years is well known.

Exiled writing is always double-edged, involving not so much nostalgia as sharp longing; not so much sentimentality as twin or, in Nazand's case, quadruple mentalities – being born and having grown up in Iraq she has Arabic and both her French and English are strong enough to self-translate – hardly surprising since she studied at the Sorbonne and has lived several years in France and translated into Kurdish T. S. Eliot and Baudelaire. She seems to have learnt from Eliot's sense of Time and her statement on the Loire river: 'This is a dry time' seems to me to be Eliotesque. One can only imagine the sheer concentration and cultural awareness necessary to translate Eliot and Baudelaire and how it would enrich Kurdish poetry and Nazand's own.

I was surprised to see that her first dissertation in 1987 at Mosul University was on men-women relationships in D.H. Lawrence's *Lady Chatterly's Lover*. She obtained her MA on the influence of English romanticism, in particular Shelley, on modern Kurdish poetry and her PhD on the image of Kurdish women in European literatures from the Sorbonne University.

Nazand is a genocide survivor; two of her brothers were executed in Saddam Hussein's prisons and her third brother who managed to flee was killed in Germany. Her father was one of the first victims of the Ba'thist regime in 1968. Nazand fled death in 1987, but did not give up hope; she obtained a scholarship from the French Foreign Ministry and continued her studies at the Sorbonne. According to Nazand "you can only overcome your pain and anger, through artistic creation, through poetry".

When you meet Nazand she is a tall, elegant, soft-spoken, calm person who can slip with ease between French and English. Her gentleness does not so much conceal her burning passion for human rights as accentuate it. She is that rare person who believes in dialogue and somehow retains respect for and from the many sides of the Kurdish question. She is one of the leaders of the campaign against honour killings and is an activist for the status of Kurdish women.

It was at a meeting of Exiled Writers' Ink that I saw the film of the poison gas massacre at Halabja, shot by an Iranian journalist. The silent camera captured fresh corpses in multicoloured clothes and zoomed into rooms where whole families lay freshly gassed. After it the poets' and writers' words, our words, seemed so inadequate to express our horror at one of the most barbarous massacres of the 20th Century, perpetrated by the perpetrator of the lesser known Anfal: Saddam Hussein.

Reader, I am not making politics – these are the universal symbols against which all modern Kurdish poems are written.

We find Nazand defending the female body in 'My Body is Mine' against the sinister *them*, which concludes 'but I was one and they were all' that has a macabre clashing ring with the musketeers' refrain: 'One for all, and all for one'. But reading these poems of Nazand it is easy for us to stand in solidarity with her. In 'Dreams' she offers: 'I reconcile God and the snake / in my dreams / I cleanse Eve's sins / and return Adam to paradise' and how poignant this is when we think now of what is happening in Iraq where the Garden of Eden (let alone the Tower of Babel) is meant to have been set. I will not reveal the secrets held or withheld in the poem 'Prayer' – but they are startling and very revelatory to those who attempt to right the world with Human Rights.

Although Nazand's poems contain many mentions of frontiers I think she should be an honorary poet of Médecins Sans Frontières: she is treating human souls in acute conditions, calmly under the fire of recent events in these elegant poems. There are many poems dedicated to her mother. The end of 'God is not dead for my mother' is a brilliant example of language having two equally powerful meanings:

when you can trace the white wings of your dead children
flying over the path of light in the azure of the sky
you don't need God to die

In the short poem 'Journey' Nazand indicates the powerful search for herself – and for expression:

I went on
Beyond things
Beyond words
Beyond the body
Beyond the wind
Then I came across myself

It is in the shortest poems that the poet is often at her most philosophical:

...Knowledge is not about knowing
but about looking through a smiling window
reflecting a different image

Even personal happiness becomes a steep climb in 'Voice': 'Happiness is a ladder / Let's climb it together.'

Richard McKane, December 2004

Contents

Exile *13*
At a Happiness Symposium in Wales *14*
The Wall *15*
Evening by the Loire *16*
Colour and Words *18*
It is Only in Love that the Body Turns into a Leaf *20*
Here Me There *21*
Two Tongues Fight *22*
Hide and Seek in Bergalu *24*
An Ordinary Day *25*
A Song for My People *26*
Ghazu *28*
Mass Grave *31*
Fireworks *32*
My Granny's Tales *33*
God is Not Dead for My Mother *34*
My Mother's Prayers *35*
My Body is Mine *38*

Celebration *40*
Silence in My Ears *42*
My Mother Pictured Amongst Tobacco Leaves *44*
A Song of a Murdered Girl *46*
A Smiling Window / Friendship *47*
Absence *48*
A Child's Painting *49*
Dreams *50*
Illusion / Prayer *52*
Voice *53*
Question *54*
Certainty *56*
Life in a Day *57*
Deliverance *58*
The War Was Over *59*
A Letter *60*
A Message *61*
Calm / Journey *62*

مەنفا

لە کۆتایی کەشتێکی کەوش
سەرەتای هەرێ تەم
پێم ئایە سەرزەمینێکی شین
لەوێ ڕاتینێکی تیشریان هەبوو دەنگەکان
مانایەکی جیا نەنگەکان
لە یەکەم شەودا پاسپۆرتە مێژوەکەم دڕاند
دەو خۆدم ناشت
کە لە سەقدە ساوەکان داڵدەی دەدام
لە خاڵەکانی پشکنین لە جیاتیم دەدوا
لەو خۆدە دڵێیەم ناشت و
بۆ ئاتی حەقیقی خۆم گریام
کە ڕۆژنک لەسەرگەردێکی نوین ونبوو
گەردنک کە چیتەر هی من نیە و
هەمیشە لە ناخدا هەناسە دەدا

لە سەرەتای فەسڵی تەم
سەرزەمینێکی شین
بە کوڵانە تەنهاکاندا دەگەڕام
من دەگەڕام بۆ زمانێکی نوێ
بۆ چنینی ستراینک بۆ هۆزنکی لانەواز
من دەگەڕام بۆ ئاوێنەرێکی دەفسوناوی
کە خۆدم سەرتاپا
نەنک بداتەوە تیایدا

12

Exile

It was the end of a cold journey
The beginning of a silent season
I arrived in a sad island
where voices had a sharp music
and colour a different meaning
I began my first night
by shredding my forged passport
burying the dual person
that had consoled me on my solitary voyage
and talked for me at check points
I buried that false self
and cried for the real one
that once was me
the self that was left behind
on a fresh silvery hill
which no longer belongs to me
but always breathes inside me

It was the beginning of a blue season
the end of a long journey
I walked down the lonely lanes
in an unknown city
in search of a new voice
to chant for a wandering nation
I was in search of a magic mirror
that could reflect my whole being

At a Happiness Symposium in Wales

A psychologist said
Graveyards may help you feel happier,
visit a graveyard when you are depressed

There is a thin line between life and death, my friend
and I am a graveyard

I am happy to be alive, my friend
After *Halabja*[1] and *Anfal*[2]
I am happy to become the voice
of a land
that contains the mass graves of our brothers

There is a thin line between life and death, my friend
There is a thin line between life and death

The Wall

I woke up one day from a deep sleep
and found myself in a cold corner of the earth
brimming with uncertainty

I looked for the soft face of the sky
for the fresh smell of the sand after summer rain
and I looked for the lullaby of the trees
the serene silhouette of mother
and the subtle silence of father
I looked for the laughter of my baby sister
and for the peaceful presence of my brother

In a cold corner of the earth
brimming with uncertainty
I found myself faced with a naked wall
the silent stone of a refugee camp
reflecting the faded face of my father
the frozen laughter of my baby sister
A naked wall was standing still
reflecting the death of our brothers
who were unable to flee
the poisoning rain in *Halabja*
to take refuge here
in this cold corner of the earth

Evening by the Loire

Alone
like many afternoons
with an old book under my arm
I walk on the shore of the Loire

And I hear them saying
This is a dry time
the Loire is no longer whistling
nor does she offer her silky flowers
to the amorous hands of the wind

And the Loire is the silhouette of a wounded season
passing by quietly

Here is a colourful group of children
throwing soft flat stones at the face of the Loire
the round lines of their instant bubbles
are the wrinkled gazes of the elderly bald women
sitting in the emptiness of the day
and dreaming of the morning of time

And the Loire is a thin lane
stretching towards a grey valley

And there are drunken men
brushing the violet dust of the years off their shoulders
and their empty bottles
are golden girdles of their solitude

And the Loire is a soft flute note
flowing smoothly

And they keep saying
This is a dry time
And the sea birds are not dancing
And the rocks are not dreaming
And the Loire is an eagle with broken wings
Passing by slowly

And I hear them saying
This is a dry time
The deep blue gaze of the Loire
an exiled poet
walking by
with an old book under her arm
saying "bonsoir" to the Loire
Disappearing...

Colour and Words[1]

1

I split myself
between colour and words
my face is fleshed out in colour
and my truth in words

2

The fingers of time
dull our clarity
only in each other
our light can be seen

3

Lines are winds
winds are lines
I am blowing towards you
and so towards myself

4

I have been
with you for a long time
and so also with myself

5

Melting into each other
transcendent like the Sufis
we tilt towards the unknowable

6

Only fingers of snow
can paint the frontier
between you and me

It is Only in Love that the Body Turns into a Leaf

It is only in love that the body turns into a leaf
and the head into an enchanting violin
you resemble the notes of Schubert
and the landscape of Van Gogh
an élan towards the azure
you are a silent scream
flying over every line
the lines of solitude
and those of unity
spilling over like a dervish
you are not here nor there
Oh my *semblable*
where are you traveling to
in this place of absence?

Here Me There

I am a white shadow
between here and there

My past
was a goddess in the East
At dawn
my mother would cover her with a veil of light
mystics would meditate on her
Mullahs feared her
At night majestically
Malak Tawus[1] held her hand
to the dome of self-knowledge
In the mornings
the young knelt to her chestnut plaits
and she
like *Inanna*[2]
inside her temple of beauty
waited for *Dumuzy*[3]

My present
is in Paris
sitting in the Grand Cluny café
with a group of men friends
discussing Jean Paul Sartre's *L'Etre et le Néant*
After a row, over *Le Deuxième Sexe* of De Beauvoir
Haval says let's go for a promenade by the Seine
walking across Le Pont Mirabeau
I meditate on time flowing under the bridge

My future
is sleeping between East and West
dreaming of both

Two Tongues Fight
After Sujata Bhatt

I grew up with two tongues
in perpetual fight
My mother tongue was a butterfly
in turquoise flight
over a valley of light
singing a melody for life
I still remember the song:

وەرە بۆ لام بفڕە بە باڵ
(Wara bo lam bfra ba bal)

من و تۆ دەبینە هەڤاڵ
(Mn u to dabina haval)[1]

My alien tongue was a snake
invading me
slithering into my body
and roaring:

امە عربیە واحدە
(Umma Arabiyah wahidah)?

دات رسالە خالدە
(That risala khalidah)[2]

My mother tongue was too high to fall
too vibrant to be silenced
My alien tongue
moved into my days
my school books
It devoured my alphabets
and occupied the white space of my childhood
A chilly wind started to blow

My mother tongue was uppermost
too vibrant to be silenced
it flew to the Zagroz[1] mountains
gathered an army of butterflies
and besieged the snaky tongue

The tongues went into perpetual battle
A battle that became
the history of a nation

Hide and Seek in Bergalu

A fresh summer morning
on the lower slopes of *Bergalu* village
two children played hide and seek
women planted trees in their garden

When a warplane roared in
rushed us face-down to the ground

After four heavy circles
and a shower of shells
a thick line of smoke
billowed from the land

Eighteen years on
on the lower slopes of a village
an old woman can be seen
circling around an empty hole
chasing the shadow of two children
playing hide and seek in *Bergalu*

An Ordinary Day

The security officer
got up early
put on his white shirt
had honey toast with nuts
kissed his three children
hugged his wife passionately
and left for work

At his desk
sat ten files
of ten men to be shot
He signed them
while drinking mint tea

At ten o'clock
he ordered the shooting
got angry over a gunman who missed his target
Taking out his pistol
he fired at the missed target ten times

Before the end of his shift
he visited the mothers of the ten shot men
ordered each to pay 100 dinars
for the cost of the bullets that killed their sons

In the evening
he celebrated his brother's birthday

At night
on the surface of a mirror
he saw a drop of blood trickling down to his feet
He tried to wash it
the trickle rose to his chest

Where does the difference lie between the killer and killed?

A Song for My People
After Octavio Paz

I am light
My echo slides down from the heights, I pour myself across your face,
I am reflected in your eyes. I lighten your stones, the primitive stones,
I trickle swiftly into your time and my stream echoes. Your drought
covers its hidden sources, I move like a golden cataract across your
landscapes, I sing under your eyelashes, I lie on your banks, your body
assumes the shape of a river, I lay my corpse across your skin

Passion of sunlight over sleeping grass

I am the light-rays of your sun
My countenance grows wings, I fly over the heights of your silence, I rain
brightness on the bells of speech, a vision blooms, sight opens its arms,
whiteness streams across your verdure, the stones turn into rainbows,
the primitive stones, I trickle swiftly into your time, my stream echoes,
your dust blooms, your sky is covered with a veil of shyness, under my
warm branches alphabets take their first step

Rhythms of colour at the door frame of life

I am the light-rays of your sun
I trickle over your body of years, I splash light under the feet of your old
age, I cradle-rock into your childhood, I rub the chest of your nights,
my palms catch fire, I catch sight of the long strands of your dreams on
the cheeks of time, I trickle swiftly into your days and my stream echoes,
the stones burst into laughter, primitive stones, time opens its arms,
I carry a basket of words, I come to tie a necklace of the future to the bare
shoulders of your present, like an autumn leaf I drift high up into the
hair-licks of cloud

You glitter there in my words

I am your light
The azure's palm is my shrine, I rise from the depths of flight. I alight on your shoulder like a *Huma*[1], your forehead blossoms stars, your face lights up like a lamp, I trickle swiftly through your time and my stream echoes. Your rocks turn into swans, your primitive stones grow wings and fly, your sky turns through its pages, a drop of blue falls at your feet, you wash yourself for prayer, an angel comes to you, I come to you like a sacred feather in a landscape of wind and smooth over your back with my angel hand, your soul overflowing, your body glowing

Beauty shimmers birdsong under the light of my holiness

O my scattered people

Ghazu[1]
To the widows of Anfal

Words started out from the sacred books
Meaning started out from the bright words
Voice started out from the hidden meaning
The voice of rage, of wretched conquest
It blew Anfal
A n f a l, A n f a l

A: is arson, the furious fire
The crackling of the children's souls
scorching of mothers' hearts
the echo of the Fall of lives

N: is Nur, the Holy Light
A prophetic beam
moving aggressively
It folds into our days
brings a desert
Pouring sands of *Ghazu* into the eyes of our springs

F: is a flame in a lantern
A lantern of waiting
glowing blue
in the hand of a saintly woman
a widow, of 16 years old
on the steps of loneliness

A: is anticipation
A hope of returning
towards the celebration of colour
A gracious hope
to illuminate hugely in their lives
to reclaim lost years
and reconcile with life

L: our luminous vision blurred
wrapping us in mist
leaving us lacerated on the edge of Holy Books

A n f a l, A n f a l
A voice blew, the voice of wretched conquest
Voice of desert storms and
tempest of Fall
It blew a voice
a voice of rage, a voice of wrath
It blew Anfal

My mother on the steps of waiting
counting her prayer beads
weaving the necklace of hope
when the body of her son
fell into her arms

A n f a l, A n f a l
It blew a voice
voice of wrath, voice of conquest
Conquest of garden,
Conquest of colour
Conquest of flight
Howls pour from the silence of waiting
No one dares say, "They are dead."
It has been 13 years that
my mother has carried the lantern of waiting
on the step of loneliness
weaving an encounter with her youngest son
Lanterns of waiting
in the hands of 50 thousand widows
in the narrow lanes of hope
The lanterns of waiting
are glowing blue
glowing blue
The lanterns of waiting

Mass Grave

The earth has stood up again
It stood up as a desert
with its face covered in red
holding a skull in its hands

The earth stood up
to speak of a child smiling
while shot to death
The earth stood up
to speak of the screams of a girl
about to be raped
The earth stood up
to speak of the prayers of an old man
being scorched
The earth stood up
to speak the words of a poet
while he was being buried alive

The earth stood up once again
It stood up to break the silence
around the burning body of Kurdistan

Fireworks
To John

The night is overflowing
the city centre radiant like an illuminated valley
and the trees full of music
and the streets a river of human beings
who dance and laugh
and in the middle
the fountain is rising proudly
to embrace the air
the enchanted gaze of the moon
and the timid smile of the stars
and the people keep dancing and singing
Suddenly midnight falls with blue sounds
and a mountain of ho ha
The sparkburst of fireworks
Rains in volcanic lines

C'est le 14 juillet
la célébration de la révolution française

And in a corner of a little room
I am crawling and shivering
my eyes closed
my hands on my ears
to avoid hearing
the echo of the past
to avoid living
the memory of the war
with the orange sounds of the bombs
falling over my childhood
in *Koysinjak*[1]

My Granny's Tales
To my late brother Qubad

On the plain of your absence
a window is opened
a window the size of the joy
of finding each other again
a window, the size of a meeting
with the past
of the serenity of my granny's tales

Life can be a purple reunion
between a sister and a brother
in the white room of words
in front of the chimney of my grandmother's wisdom

And then she is saying
Life can be a blue waiting
for love or for departure
for the birth of a vision
or a dissolving in the sand
life can be blue waiting
for the everlasting loss of someone
and the beginning of the end
the end of togetherness
the beginning of a habit

Life can be only a habit
a habit of being together
or of facing the distance
a habit of absence
and of the cold face of the years
a habit of another waiting
waiting for the opening of a new window
the size of our reunion

God is Not Dead for My Mother

"Truth is an illusion"
said Nietzsche

For my mother who has never been to school
truth is standing up calmly
after a deluge
planting a garden
with serene hands
speaking the language of trees
and understanding the alphabet of rain

For my mother truth is
reading the silence of my brothers' faces
as they lie in stone
and seeing in the blueness of the sky
a plume of light tracing a path
which stretches deep
beyond the cloud and the stars

When you can trace the white wings of your dead children
flying over the path of light in the azure of the sky
you don't need God to die

My Mother's Prayers

Let's light up a cigarette
light a candle
and start dancing, my friend
Let's sing to calm down the daisies
and console my mother's lonely prayers

My mother is praying every morning
Instead of two *Rikat*[1]
she kneels six times
She prays for the safety of our garden
and calls on God to protect the family

My friend
Let's listen to the prayers of my mother
Let's see how she sighs
and turns around and around
She calls on the birds to fly her sons across borders
She begs the wind to wrap itself around her baby daughter
and shield her from the rain of poisoning gas

Let's drink a cup of wine my friend
and fly over the highlands
let's familiarize ourselves with heights
and look down at the falling stars

My mother has prayed
and cried six times
Her wishes glitter like diamonds
under the light of faith
take steps and climb over cloud-hills to the sky
where instead of flying
they fall down on the sand

My mother is praying every morning
instead of two *Rikat*
she kneels
and cries six times
she turns around and around
she calls on God to keep our garden safe
to protect us from calamity
from the apocalypse
My mother's prayers grow old
her fresh wishes grow old
from flying over the seasons
returning to our homeland
and landing on a field of daisies

My friend, let's dance together
we know that the time for prayer is over
the wings of flight have been shredded
the lips of the wind have dried
the plaits of the sun have been cut off
the fingers of the rain have been burnt
and the memory of the garden has perished
We know my friend
that the time of prayer has gone
the birds have showered down
the ladders have fainted

My mother's prayer mat is the colour of the sky
and her prayers the colour of autumn
Our garden is tired
the butterflies pale

Let's build a shelter in loneliness, my friend
redress the ladders
and steal back light from shadows

Let's collect seeds from my mother's prayers
my friend
and sow them
under the leaves in the pale garden
Maybe lovers will walk by here one day
and hang wishes in the trees

Nothing consoles my mother's soul
apart from one tiny wish
the wish for afterlife
She dreams of getting up in the other world
and walking down the blue lanes of paradise
meeting again with her sons
holding the hands of her baby daughter
hugging her brothers
who left on a journey of faith
and were never seen again

My mother prays for a smooth walk
from the desert of being
to the shore of nothingness
She visits the tombs of her sons
and prays for the safety of their souls

My friend, let's dance together
Let's escape from this time of deception
The time for prayer has passed

My Body is Mine

A white territory
crossed by green lines
my body grew softly

Soon the lines made frontiers
between me and my dreams
between me and my pleasure

First it was my mother
who innocently
threw me into the hands of a witch
and announced: "let her be blessed for ever"
A red stream flowed from my south

One night
in the yard of my childhood
I heard the whisper of a hand
trying to sing on my shores
in the froth of waves
a garden grew on the sand
Then the song woke them up
and they decided to cut my limbs
A red river flooded towards my east

And then a breeze of laughter
touched my hair
it illuminated my face
enchanted me
a fountain was born
like a symphony in the air
and it woke *them* up
and they decided to cut my lips
A red torrent flooded into my west

A soldier walked into my garden
picked my white lilac
they saw him killing my colours
and they said it was my fault
and I was given away to an old man
who dried up my source
and poured darkness over my youth
A red ocean deluged my north
I became a widow at the age of twelve

When reconciled to myself
I planted a young tree
Freedom
But I was one
and they were all

Celebration

1

A piece of shadow
fell to my feet
It divided space
and grew frontiers
I am here and beyond at the same time
but always with you

2

This place is full of uncertainty
A shadow of silence lies
on the cheeks of togetherness
Our hands are full of mist

3

The sunlight resembles us
her voice is stable
and like us she is fragile
like us she is strong
like us she cries in silence

4

Exile, like grass
grew softly
between our hands

5

This is not the end of the road
it is the end of the beginning
the paths ended here
but they restart from this end

6

Together or separate
we rewrite each other
as we were in the past
not in our future

7

One morning, afternoon or evening
we will fall down in silence
Our eyes closed as if we're asleep
we will breathe like the dead

Silence in My Ears
After 'Ash Wednesday' by T.S. Eliot

No longer
The beauty of moments captures me no longer
No more desire
The silence of feet
in my ears
I don't wish to hear it any longer
for these feet cannot walk any more
like weights
they only hit the earth

When looking behind
I see a dazzling child
on the palm of the snow
playing with the sun's rays

Passing by
I see a fretful girl
gathering pieces of words
on the face of the years
she kneels to *Haji*[1]
and dresses her hair with star-poems

A radiant woman
meditates on the hours
Leaves fade
Her body wrinkles
The old eagle does not open its wings any more
No more desire
The beauty of moments does not capture me any more
The silence of feet
in my ears
I don't wish to hear any more
for these feet cannot walk any longer
like weights
they only hit the earth

My Mother Pictured Amongst Tobacco Leaves

Your picture in the greenness of the tobacco leaves
reflecting the light of the Orient
you bend among the endless lines
of the staring tobacco plants
like doubt after conviction
you pick up the leaves
lay them in the *Charoga*[1]
hanging at your neck
and carry them to the *Ber Heywan*[2]

Piles of sad leaves
Piles of silence
hidden under the *Nur*[3] of the Orient

Your wrinkled hands
talk to me
tell the story of a stolen childhood
the loneliness of women in my homeland

I look at your fingers
you place the leaves one by one on the tobacco *shish*
threading them like long beads into a necklace
then you kneel before the heap of tobacco necklaces
place them on your back,
climb the hill to reach the *Chardagh*[4]
and hang them in precise lines
to dry

Infinite lines of tobacco necklaces
Infinite scars on your heart

I can feel your body drying up
like the tobacco plant in the midsummer heat
and your life
your life similar to the tobacco leaves
has been picked and burnt away
like a cigarette
between a man's fingers

A Song of a Murdered Girl[1]
To the victims of honour crimes

Hey hey hey hey
My life story may one day become yours

My story
is the tale of a flower
a white lilac in a corner of the earth
smiling, gracious
the friend of beauty

One day a wind blew
a grey, heavy long-clawed wind
heavy as the weight
of the sin of being
the sin of being a woman

Hey hey hey hey
I was a white lilac
a friend of the rain
I was love
The grey, heavy long-clawed wind
blew at me
it came closer and
closer to me
in a man's face
and broke my stars
The grey, heavy long-clawed wind
with a man's face
came closer and
closer to me
put its claws at my cheeks
strangled my butterflies
and cut the throat of my light

Hey hey hey hey
My life story may one day become yours

A Smiling Window

In a corner of loneliness
I slept with words

How our days are
illuminated by poetry!

And then I heard a voice
in the greenness of the grass
saying: Knowledge is not about knowing
but about looking through a smiling window
reflecting a different image

Friendship

A living softness
A sublime depth
Limitless pleasure
Is our measure
In our moments together

Absence

To my brothers who are
no longer in this world

I can see you, brothers
such statues of silk
your hands holding the stars
your bodies are the dust
How infinitely you stretch out!

Your voices are colourless
your colourlessness is silent
and your silence is as high as your absence

In a cascade of blue sorrow
you pour certainty onto our palms
under your holy light
we walk through a mirror
truth blinks its eyes
and wisdom has an afternoon nap
a flock of sin takes flight
the past is a desolate land
the present is your soundless hands
and the future is sand

A Child's Painting
On a drawing by my 3 year-old son

A blue line
is bending
it turns towards you
an arrow facing the south
what does it tell you, mother?

My life is full of circles
and they are intermingled
a black point in the centre
tells of departure

All signs bend towards you
to the early days
the colours of the lines are magic
my smile is bright
in the arms of you mother
and you father

The blue line is life
when my father climbed up
nothing happened
when you wanted to climb higher
into your own life
I was left alone, mother

Dreams

I'd like to follow in the footsteps of my dreams
to frame my present from my dreams
to plant my words
in their soil
to wear a necklace of dream-stars
to link up with the moon
and to fly blue in space

The past with its clawed fists
the present with its idiotic grimness
the future with its doubts and secrets
where do they take me?
A time of rust!

Lifetime, Desire, Stone
Everything has its own defined space
everything has its own colour and dullness
everything but dreams
indefinite, mysterious, timeless
Do you not hear the footsteps of your dreams?
Do you not hear the murmur of their breath?
They walk beside you,
lie next to you,
are always conceived within you
with seeds of unforeseen joy
I'd like to follow in the footsteps of my dreams

In dreams I map out a space
in dreams I eat an apple from the garden of Eden
I turn into an angel
I reconcile God and the snake

in my dreams
I cleanse Eve's sins
and return Adam to Paradise

In my dreams I become a mirage
hold the hand of the rain
and release it over the desert
in dreams
I become morning dew glinting on the eyelashes of the sand

In dreams I approach my soul
become a cataract of light
cross all the remote distances
and engrave the words of a poem on the rocks of Judaea

I'd like to follow in the footsteps of my dreams
transform myself into words
steal myself into poetry
Look, I am wearing my necklace of words

In dreams I steal back from words to myself

Illusion

I placed a yellow leaf
on the white wings of the wind
and let it go
then I heard a melody in the air:
"Exile will promise me
a turquoise land
and a wise tribe
where I am myself
and freedom is the friend of human beings"

Prayer[1]

In a desert
at the foot of the cloud-hills
under the shadow of the wind
a woman stood up
a slender being
who turned her face to God
a face full of doubts
She lifted her hands
and I heard her pray:

"Oh my Lord
grant me the power
to avoid understanding your secrets
for I don't want to be shattered by anger"

Voice

Are you happy?
asked a sorrowful voice
through a lonely door

It came closer
and closer through the sad doorway
and said softly:
Life is a battle
but happiness is an instant
you have to catch
Happiness is beauty
you have to taste
Happiness is affection
you have to share
Happiness is conviction
you have to create
Happiness is speech
you have to articulate
Happiness is a ladder
let's climb it together.

A warm voice
from the sorrowful doorway
repeated these words

Question

When I was a child
I could see the beauty of daisies
in my own fingers
In the greenness of the Sewan Vineyard
I would read my first lesson
gently stretch my fingers
and pluck a flower:
"I will pass – I won't
I will pass – I won't"

The petals like butterflies
coquettish and joyful
would settle on the peaceful grass

I was a child
and could see the beauty of daisies
in my fingers

When I was a teenager
the lessons were wind
flying in love
they were circling around my body
I would stretch my fingers
and pluck a flower:
"Loves me – loves me not
he loves me – he loves me not"
The petals like the snowflakes
dancing and playful
would rain on the indulgent grass

I was still a child
could see the beauty of daisies
in my fingers

Now on the threshold of winter
after travelling in many countries
learning many lessons
the daisy petals sorry and regretful
breathe slowly in the folds of my fingers:
"Will I return home? Will I return? Will I?

Certainty

The secrets are calling for us
hide me in the infinity of your heart
let the darkness of things
not be lines between us
let the lines
not be frontiers of forgetting

I sat down by the side of the sun
Oh, how warm is closeness!
How close is togetherness
in the arms of words
and the embrace of certainty

Life in a Day

I was born
one morning with the dawn
The sun put a necklace of beams around my neck
and the stream in front of my birth garden
handed me a present of water

At noon
I immersed myself in the river of my childhood farm
Shakhi Mishka
Racing down the spring-golden hills
I wore rose water
tied a *wanawsha* leaf in my hair

Towards the afternoon
I went with my friend
to the shores of the Tigris
Kisses, poems
became rowing boats
transporting us towards
the beaches of *volupté*

After the sunset
face down
we found that we had been pushed
to the edge of the Atlantic Ocean
Together
we built two tombs in the sand
and wrote "Time"

Deliverance

My body is quiet as a fall of snow
my spirit, a stream

I remember those who passed by here once
crossed the line of light in the sky
and never came back again
I remember them and meditate on the grandeur of the sun
I remember them and listen to the wonder of the breeze
I remember them and touch the silence of the stone
I remember them and I can see my pain turn into a ball of cotton
blown away on the wind

The War Was Over

Christmas Day
I arrived at my mother's house
with my four-year-old son
That was their first encounter

My son had seen her photographs
and jumped into her arms
My mother was struggling to hide her tears

No-one will know
if they were tears of joy
or of grief for the loss of my brother
who carried the same name

In deep silence
still in her arms
Nawzad smiled and said:
I have missed you Nana giyan

A Letter

From a crowded street
I stepped into a gallery
saw the painting of Time, my dear
the dictator time

Hours, minutes, seconds
Our days

An elderly woman standing
in front of the painting
began to cry
and fell down
A child hurried to pick up her cane
We too grow old, my dear
we too will fall

A Message

A crystal bottle in the sea
I walk through time

In the beginning
there was a meeting
A man and a woman wrote a message
put it in a crystal bottle
and with care
placed it in the hands of the sea

My body grew under the caress of the wind
it floated harmoniously
in cold and heat
it never stopped
A crystal bottle
holding a message
gliding in the hands of the sea

One evening it landed on a southern coast
a dark-haired child unscrewed it
and read:

"Life is a sea
only through love
can it hold me in its heart"

Calm

Let's lie down
close our eyes
and listen to the music of the sun
to the grass singing
Let words have a rest
and speech a little siesta

Journey

I walked in the land of souls
and in the distance
I saw myself
a watery sky
full of darting little fishes
I went on
beyond things
beyond words
beyond the body
beyond the wind
Then I came across myself

page 14
1. *Halabja* is the name of a Kurdish town subjected to chemical bombardment in 1988 by the Iraqi army under the regime of Saddam Hussein. Five thousand civilians died in the space of one day. The area and the survivors suffer to this day from the consequences of the chemical gas.
2. *Anfal* is the name of a genocidal campaign carried out by the Ba'thist regime of Iraq against Kurdish civilians at the end of the 80s. The word has been taken from the Holy Quran, meaning pillaging and sacking the "infidels". Over 100,000 people died and 182,000 disappeared in the operation. There are more than 50,000 widows of *Anfal* in the Kurdistan region who still wait for their deported beloved to come back.

page 18
1. These poems are written on six paintings by the Kurdish artist, Rebwar Saed, as part of a project called *Colour and Words*.

page 21
1. The Yezidis prophet, a pre-monotheist religion in Kurdistan.
2. *Innana* became Ishtar. She was the Goddess of Love during the Sumerian epoch. She is considered the most important Goddess in Mesopotamia, with many temples built in her honour, including one in *Arbail* (*Erbil* in Iraqi Kurdistan of today).
3. *Dumuzy* became Tumuz. He was the lover of *Innana* and he was responsible for promoting fertility.

page 22
1. From a Kurdish children's song: "Come and fly towards me, You and I will become friends."
2. A pan-Arab slogan of the Ba'th party: "There is one Arab nation, it has an eternal message"

page 23
1. A chain of high mountains across Kurdistan.

page 27
1. *Huma* in Kurdish and Iranian mythology is a mythical bird that brings luck and privilege to people.

page 28
1. *Ghazu* is a classic Arabic word which means *conquest*.

page 32
1. *Koysinjak* is the name of Nazand's home town.

page 35
1. Kneeling in Islamic prayer.

page 42
1. Refers to the great XIX century Kurdish poet Haji Qadri Koyi who comes from *Koysinjak*.

page 44
1. *Charoga* is a sling put around the neck to put tobacco leaves in.
2. *Ber Heywan* is a courtyard.
3. *Nur* is light, in religious terms it is divine light.
4. *Chardagh* is the place where tobacco is hung in lines to dry.

page 46
1. This poem was written on 8 March 2000 and read on the occasion of the launch of *Kurdish Women Action against Honour Killing* (KWAHK).

page 52
1. Inspired by a Chinese proverb: "If you understand all the injustice of the world, you risk dying of anger."

Nazand Begikhani was born in Kurdistan (Iraq) in 1964. She has been living in exile (Denmark, France and later UK) since 1987. She took her first degree in English language and literature, then completed an MA and PhD in comparative literature at the Sorbonne. She published her first poetry collection *Yesterday of Tomorrow* in Paris in 1995. Her second collection *Celebrations* was published in Kurdistan by Arras in 2004. Arras also published her third collection *Colour of Sand* in 2005. *Bells of Speech* is her first collection in English.

She is a polyglot and translates her own poetry into French and English. Many of her poems are published in French, Arabic, Persian and English. She has also translated Baudelaire and Eliot into Kurdish.

Apart from writing poetry, Nazand is an active researcher and advocate for women's human rights. She is a founding member and co-ordinator of the network organisation Kurdish Women Action against Honour Killing (KWAHK). Her research on Kurdish gender is widely published in Kurdish, but also in French and English.